CHANGING LIVES
ONE NOTE AT A TIME

The Ministry of Note Writing

CAROL ANN MC GIFFIN

Inspiring Voices®
A Service of **Guideposts**

All Scripture quotations are taken from the New International Version 1984

Illustrations by Peggy Hunter.

Inspiring Voices books may be ordered through booksellers or by contacting:

Inspiring Voices
1663 Liberty Drive
Bloomington, IN 47403
www.inspiringvoices.com
1-(866) 697-5313

ISBN: 978-1-4624-0028-7 (sc)
ISBN: 978-1-4624-0027-0 (e)

Library of Congress Control Number: 2011940550

Printed in the United States of America

Inspiring Voices rev. date: 10/25/2011

CHANGING LIVES

ONE NOTE AT A TIME

Thankful Words

"When I see an envelope with your name on it, I'm pleased for I know there is an uplifting message inside." An older adult

"You have no idea how much your notes have helped me through my difficult times." A pianist

"God has given you a wonderful gift of caring, and sharing it with others. Don't every stop using it. You don't know how much it meant to me." A cancer victim

"You have taught me that the written word is ultimately as important, if not more important, than the spoken word." A co-worker

"I like the way God is always in your mind when you write." An older adult

"Thank you for reminding me that words from the heart have much value." A friend

"I have been asking God how He could use me. When you spoke at the Refresher Weekend, I realized that was the answer." A young mother

"I love reading through your book filled with encouragement. Every time I read it I try to send an encouraging note to someone. Thank you." A church worker

"I am so impressed by your ministry it has encouraged me to write more notes to my friends and relatives." A single adult

Contents

For

My family of friends
who have helped me through the steps of my life …
I CELEBRATE YOU!

My wonderful husband, Jerry,
best friend of all

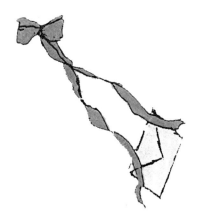

"He who refreshes others will himself be refreshed."
Proverbs 11:25

Foreword

In the corner of my studio sits a beautifully decorated box full of treasures. Not the gold and silver kind, but treasures of the heart ... the riches of God's love and grace, comfort and encouragement, hope and blessing, poured out to me through hand-written notes from family, friends, and even strangers over the years and for various reasons. These are the treasures Carol writes about in the pages of this book.

I have known Carol as a friend for several years and have been personally encouraged through her note-writing ministry. Carol knows and understands, through her own life experience, the power of a hand-written note to not only touch the heart of the receiver but to potentially have a life-changing impact.

God has truly given Carol the gift of knowing how to encourage others in every season of life—in times of celebration and in times of great pain—and she gracefully shares her wisdom and insights with us in the pages of this little book. I am confident her words of encouragement and her heartfelt examples will inspire you ... and empower you ... to pick up that pen and allow God to use you to encourage others as He has her.

Karla Dornacher
Author and Artist
www.karladornacher.typepad.com

Preface

Ministry, you say? Writing notes is a ministry?

The apostle Paul provides a list of spiritual gifts in Romans 12. Go down the list and stop at "encourage." "*If it is encouraging, let him encourage.*" All believers are admonished to encourage. In Hebrews 3:13 Paul wrote, "*But encourage one another daily.*"

There are many ways to encourage someone—talking to them face-to-face, calling, emailing, helping … and then there's writing. I've been encouraged in all these ways, but my heart responds most readily when I see a hand-written note to me.

Words are shared differently in a note. In the movie *Skylark*, Sarah says, "Sometimes what people choose to write down on paper is more important than what they say." People express things in ways they wouldn't or couldn't if they were talking.

There's just something special about a hand-written note that expresses God's love and directs your focus to His care over you. My pastor, Michael Trammell, put it this way, "A note lifts spirits and edifies the body of Christ."

Encouraging through note writing is a ministry … a ministry that can change a life. I invite you to take a closer look and discover within yourself the means to encourage by writing a note.

Introduction

I received a compliment from a lady I was encouraging through note writing. Rebecca wrote, "Corrie ten Boom once said that the best lessons are learned in the hardest class. I know your sensitivity to the hurt of others was shaped in one of those classrooms."

My mind immediately focused on a period of time when God reshaped my life. Years of heartbreaking trials molded my thinking to God's. Through despondency and depression I learned that God is faithful in caring for His children. Rebecca was right: my best lessons were learned in the hardest class.

One of the lessons I learned is the need to reach out and encourage people. God used that lesson to propel me into a ministry of note writing. Why notes, you might ask? Notes were the instrument God used to encourage me through my difficult times. I received encouragement and care from others through their notes to me. The notes were filled with words that touched my heart. They changed my outlook towards life completely.

Can a simple note do that?—change a life? Yes, it can. Notes can change the world for the person receiving one.

In "Basics of Note Writing," you'll find questions and answers about note writing that will encourage you to become a note writer. Each chapter will move you closer to the realization that a note is important in encouraging hearts. And you will be encouraged along the way to take that step.

In "Situations of Life," you'll find sample sentences to draw from to help you write notes for different circumstances of life. The samples can be used as they are, or you can flavor them with your own creativity. There is a short introduction to each life situation before the samples are provided. These words will help you identify the situation someone may be going through.

Look for the two "Notes for You" after each chapter. Each "Notes for You" was written by me to one woman over the course of a year. It was a special assignment from God to encourage her. Below each note are the thoughts behind the words, explaining why I wrote the words I did. It is my hope that your heart is encouraged by each note you read.

This book is filled with stories and instructions, and sample notes to help get you started. The examples are words God has given me to share with others through many years of note writing.

I invite you to come along with me on a journey of writing notes. You'll find the words in this booklet are not profound … just simple words to encourage, like the ones you'll write one day. I challenge you to start now!

Basics of Note Writing

The Worth of a Note

Some of my favorite memories include receiving notes at different times in my life. Several notes are very special to me, yet one in particular comes to mind.

Struggling through the heartbreaking trial of divorce, I felt ashamed. Attending church services was uncomfortable. Everyone knows. Disheartening thoughts plagued me. "Am I an outcast? Should I break all ties and move on?"

Then the note arrived. The author wasn't a friend of mine, but I knew her well enough to speak to her when we passed in the hall at church. "We've seen a number of people leave because of the problem you're going through," Alice wrote. "Please don't leave. Stay with us. We love you."

What a precious memory. What a life-changing moment. Somebody cared about me and was willing to write a note to tell me. She wasn't a close friend or family member—merely an acquaintance. But that short message from a willing heart changed my entire outlook. Alice noticed my situation and responded to it. The impression it made on me has lasted to this day.

Notes are special: simple expressions of encouragement and care; two or three sentences from one heart to another. That's all it takes, an honest expression of compassion.

Notes are an excellent tool of encouragement. You can hold them in your hands. If you forget what was written, you can read them again. They're always available to remind you that someone cares, and they last forever. Notes go right to the heart and that makes a lasting impression.

Re-reading a note is always refreshing. I feel better and my outlook improves.

Why write a note? Because notes have a unique way of giving a person value. As you share your thoughts with one person and tell him or her that you care, strength to endure is transmitted from the pen of one hand to the eyes of another.

My life was changed by the note Alice sent me. It helped me to see through my heartbreak and focus on encouraging words. All it took was one note.

Just one note. The kind of note that you can write.

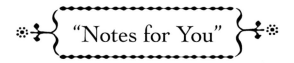
"Notes for You"

1 Thessalonians 5:24, says: "The one who calls you is faithful and he will do it." It is wonderful to know in your heart—to be absolutely certain, without a doubt—that God is faithful. I hope you have that assurance in your heart. We are failed every day, mostly by people, sometimes by circumstances, and those failures can be a weight in our hearts. But there is one who never fails us, who is always with us and who never gives up on us. "The one who calls you is faithful." I'm so glad!

It all comes down to my relationship with God. Is it strong or weak? Sure or wavering? When something happens that makes no sense, can I turn to the One who knows all?

With the assurance that God is with me, I can get through any situation. Assurance means having the confidence of knowing something is true. I either have it or I don't. There's no in-between.

I believe that all things happen for good according to God's plan. Because of what Jesus did for me, His blood covers my sin as white as snow. I can see God through Jesus, because of His love. With complete trust in God's Word, it's easier to accept things I don't understand. And that happens a lot.

My husband, Jerry, and I prayed for five years that he would be hired to oversee all maintenance work at a camp we supported. The dream came true and we were ecstatic. But during the first six weeks of employment, Jerry knew he could not work there, and resigned.

Those were stressful days. Without God's assurance that all things work for good it would have been difficult to go on. But because we knew of His faithfulness, we were able to pick up the pieces and continue moving forward.

His word is faithful. Having that assurance makes all the difference.

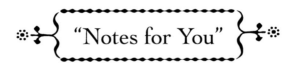

"Notes for You"

One thing I know is God answers prayer. It may take a week, a month, or years—and the answer may be far different from one I imagined—but I know God answers prayer. I have confidence in my prayers to God, as well as the prayers of faithful believers who pray on my behalf. I have confidence in the only One who is in control—our loving God.

From the very day I asked Jesus to come into my heart, to just yesterday, when He answered my request for help, I know God answers prayer.

Sometimes it's an earnest prayer I say during the day to get me through a meeting I must attend. I whisper a brief request for controlled emotions, or help with information I need to share.

Oftentimes it's a plea I express for someone who is sick or heartbroken and in need of God's care and comfort. Sometimes answers come in a timely fashion, and God's work is played out before my eyes.

Then there are the prayers that linger on for years. They weigh heavily on my mind, even though I know God is in control. I've seen answers to some of these prayers and others I still wait on today. After thirty years of walking with God I've learned not to be anxious. The answer may be hidden to my eyes, but I still have full confidence in God's purpose.

Prayer is our avenue to God. Anytime. Anywhere. I pray while I drive … iron clothes … read a book … and talk with friends. God is available and that's the way I want to be for Him!

Looking for a Need

For a number of weeks during prayer meeting, a man I didn't know requested prayer for his wife, Susan. I didn't know Susan, but there was a tug in my heart to write her a note.

Within a week after sending the note, I received a gracious letter sharing how thoughtful and appreciated my note was. The letter was full of kind words and thankfulness. I wondered which one of us benefitted more.

It's amazing how the simplest act will make a significant difference in another person's life. It did in Susan's. We never know when it will happen. We must be open to finding a need, and then we must respond to it.

Where is that person? If you share a common interest with a group of people, you've found a great place to look. A person in need will be there. Look around and listen. When your attention is drawn to listening for a need, you're usually not disappointed.

You can find many people in your inner circle of friends, and in your family, who could use an encouraging word. But, as in Susan's case, you don't need to know the person you write to.

In my year of weekly notes to one woman, I provided encouragement to someone I didn't know. The discipline of commitment in my own life was strengthened due to this task.

Finding a person to write to is easy. There are endless situations and opportunities from everyday life. *"Thinking of you ... surgery ... death ... congratulations ... divorce ... birth"*—and the list goes on and on.

Everyone needs encouragement, during both happy times and sad times. You can be the person to make a difference. Open your eyes and ears as you go about your daily life. That person is out there. Bring that person the encouragement that may change his or her life.

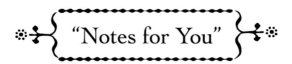

"Notes for You"

As God covered the land with snow last week, creating a picture–perfect scene, so our sins are as white as snow because of our Savior, Jesus. "Though your sins are like scarlet, they shall be as white as snow." (Isaiah 1:18b). Snow is beautiful to watch as it falls and covers the earth; and greater still is God's love that envelops His children.

I seriously pray for snow in wintertime. I love watching it fall! Being caught indoors, unexpectedly, as the world slows down for awhile is what I call a "free" day.

A free day means my work place is closed, and I can relax at home. It means the day is completely unplanned, and I can do whatever I want.

That usually means curling up on the couch, hot chocolate in hand, a good book—you know the feeling. And that's how I felt while I watched the snow fall last week.

Since I moved to the country some years ago, snow has taken on a completely different meaning for me besides declaring a free day. Water. Well water. With a good snow the ground is moistened and water levels improve.

My love of snow has taken on a more meaningful understanding than just beauty. Snow helps sustain the ground that brings our food, and fills my well. And the image of God making our sins "white as snow" leaves me with a beautiful picture of His purity.

My sin is ever before me. I go to the throne of grace often to be covered as white as snow. Sometimes it's hard to accept forgiveness, knowing how ugly my sin is. But by the grace given to me, I am covered by the brightness of His love. Snow. What a beautiful expression of His love.

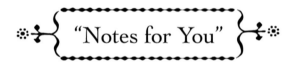

"Notes for You"

I enjoy the poems of Helen Steiner Rice. In this season of spring, when we enjoy the fragrance and beauty of flowers, let these words from her poem, "Flowers Leave Their Fragrance on the Hand that Bestows Them" inspire you to stop and smell the roses. "And you can't pluck a rose, All fragrant with dew, Without part of its fragrance Remaining with you." As you give your joy of Christ to others, may your heart overflow with the sweet fragrance of His love.

You know the feeling. You've done something for someone and they smile. It's intoxicating!

I enjoy making dates with friends—old and new. Whether it's for breakfast, lunch or dinner, I meet with a person for the sole objective of encouraging them. We may not be close friends before a date, but a warm and special relationship will begin that will last a long time.

Most new friends I meet with are pleasantly surprised with the invitation. They always end the date with comments like *"This was so much fun. We must do this again."* When God leads me to a lady to befriend, I'm always a little nervous whether they'll accept my invitation. But I haven't been refused so far, and don't expect I ever will be.

Many of these dates become annual celebrations. From each date friendship grows stronger. It may never go any farther than one date a year, but that one date opens the door to trust and acceptance. The relationship can last through years.

This is a small thing to do, but it takes time. If making dates with others is too time consuming for you, invite someone to your home, or call them. It may be just what is needed.

My dates are little flowers I give to my friends filled with the fragrance of Christ.

Giving God's Comfort

The prognosis wasn't good. Mr. White suffered a second heart attack and there were many problems associated with his health. Jerry and I wrote several notes to him and his wife, Eleanor, to let them know we cared. After a short time, Mr. White died.

Yesterday, three months after his death, Jerry and I received a card from Eleanor. "To two special friends" the outside read. On the inside Eleanor had written a dear note to us, thanking us for the encouragement and care we'd given them.

We had not known this couple until shortly before Mr. White's illness. But we had touched their hearts by sharing with them during this difficult time. After Mr. White's death, we continued to write to Eleanor.

Although Jerry and I have both lost close family members through death, it was still difficult finding the right words to share. The notes we wrote spoke of our care and concern. We offered simple words of hope.

As each of us go through difficult situations, God teaches us to trust Him for our comfort and guidance. We learn how to rest in His care and fully rely on Him to help us through each trial.

In His Word, God specifically speaks about this in 2 Corinthians 1:3: "Praise be to the God and Father of our Lord Jesus Christ, the Father of compassion and the God of all comfort, who comforts us in all our troubles, so that we can comfort those in any trouble with the comfort we ourselves have received from God."

It is through difficult times that we draw the strength and wisdom to share with others in their time of need. For Eleanor, we learned of her needs by talking with her friends and reading articles on widowhood.

Another situation difficult to write about is divorce. Barbara was separated from her husband and they eventually divorced. She's the sister of friends of ours. I did not know her personally, but I started writing notes to her. I didn't have solutions, but I understood her need since I also had suffered through divorce. What I did have was a caring heart.

The notes were frequent, every three or four weeks. I still send her notes today. Over the course of several years, Barbara has become a cherished friend … and a mutual encourager. Just the other night she called to say she was writing to a young woman.

Whether it's death, divorce, or any major occurrence in a person's life, we have the assurance of God's Word to help us comfort and embrace others. We don't have to be afraid of the tragedies in life. We can help people go through these trying times by sharing a kind word.

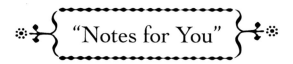
"Notes for You"

I had another free day as the snow fell last Friday. While sitting in my writing room enjoying the winter scene outside the window, I quickly grabbed my camera to capture the special moment on film. Later, I went to get the mail and found my neighbor's mail in our box. I walked to their home to deliver it and soon found myself walking home hugging a container of warm homemade soup. This simple act of kindness warmed my heart. The small acts of kindness—within every person's reach to do—are what blessings are made of.

That container of soup was just right. It not only tasted good, it satisfied my heart—an unexpected kindness. And later that day, a loaf of warm bread straight from the oven arrived at our door from another neighbor. We ate like kings!

It's the small gestures one makes that impact a life—the phone call ... the note ... the visit ... the food—showing compassion and concern.

On my job, when a meeting is planned, we serve lunch for the people attending. If it's my meeting, I order lunch, get it ready to serve, and clean up afterwards.

Recently, I was pulled in every direction, with not enough hands to do the work. When I finally got down to the kitchen to clean up, everything was done. Gail, my co-worker, knew I was busy and took care of the clean-up for me. This small kindness saved me thirty minutes and allowed me to complete another project that was waiting.

Small kindnesses make a big difference, and they're so easy to give.

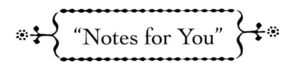

"Notes for You"

"For where your treasure is, there your heart will be also" (Matthew 6:21). Our treasure is Jesus Christ, the Good Shepherd. Our hearts can find peace in Him, as His words bring us rest. "Be at rest once more, O my soul, for the Lord has been good to you" (Psalm 116:7).

What treasures do I have here on earth? I have delightful baskets I collect and decorate my home with. The articles I've written and seen published that now hang on my writing room wall. The notes I've received that cheered my heart.

Yes, they're nice to enjoy and they make me smile, but they don't bring rest to my soul. The only treasure that can satisfy my soul is Jesus. He's the perfect gift from a loving God who wants my soul to rest in Him.

"Be at rest once more." These words have caused me to slow down and consider God's goodness many times.

Whenever I become involved in a situation that is upsetting, and I don't know what to do, I remember. I remember God's gift of salvation through Jesus. I remember the forgiveness He gives me every day as I lay my sin at the feet of His Son. I remember that one day I will be with Him in heaven because of His grace and mercy. And then my soul rests.

Many times I've tried to go forward on my own efforts, but that is going forward without God's support, without His direction. I must stop and rest. Only then will my way be smooth.

My heart is right where I want it—in the treasure chest of God.

Keep Those Notes Coming

LeAnne suffered from an eating disorder. Her family had been dealing with her illness for over a year when I first learned of the situation. LeAnne was a young girl, just out of high school. We had never met.

I started sending LeAnne a note every two to three weeks and continued doing so for a year. There were very few good reports those months, so encouraging words were hard to find.

Two years have now passed. LeAnne has not overcome her illness but has a good understanding of her problem. She's still capable of slipping into a harmful state, but she's working hard every day to overcome. I send her a note or card every other month to let her know I'm thinking of her and praying for her.

Many trials such as LeAnne's carry on for years. A person is surrounded by friends and loved ones at the beginning of a trial, but as time passes people tend to forget that the problem is still there, or they become discouraged when they see no improved results.

It's important to remember someone over the course of time. Every bit of encouragement that's instilled in a person's heart will provide needed strength and help. I still send Eleanor, whose husband died, cards at holidays, especially Valentine's Day.

Different situations make it hard to suggest how often you should write. Sometimes one or two brief notes will be sufficient, while, at other times, a dozen notes, spanning a year, may be necessary. I find myself writing four to six notes for someone recovering from an illness or surgery.

Easiest to write are notes that comfort through brief periods of illness and disappointment. Writing one or two notes to a friend who has the flu, or four or five notes to someone recovering from an operation does wonders to lift their spirits.

Separation and divorce, or a family difficulty, are situations that never seem to end and can wear down the threads of a person's life. I'm compelled not to forget those caught in lingering trials. I clearly remember my own trials, which lasted several years. The pain doesn't end after a few months of encouragement.

To help me remember when I last wrote to an individual, I keep an "Encouragement Notebook." I use a stenographer's pad, which can be purchased at any drug store or office supply store. I record who I wrote to, the date, and whether I sent a note, card, or letter or made a telephone call.

This is also a good resource that helps me remember to keep in touch with friends. Time goes by quickly. I can easily review who I've written to and decide if anyone needs a note. Keeping track of your notes will also help you remember your commitment.

As you begin writing notes and become tuned in to the concerns around you, the appropriate number of notes to write will not be a question. Your heart is a great guide!

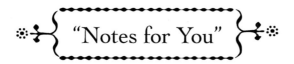

"Notes for You"

Last week I was reading Psalm 119 and was impressed how often these words appear: "for I have put my hope in your word." I believe the Bible is God's Word; I hope in it and have confidence because of it. I often pray, "I have no other hope except Thy Word, and I am comforted."

God's hope. It's gotten me through many hurricanes in my life. Each morning for many years I would pray: "I don't know what is happening, but You do, and my hope is in You."

One horrific hurricane, whose winds still bring turbulence in my life, involves my daughter. She's chosen to live a lesbian life, against my beliefs. How does one survive storms that leave an open wound in the heart—the very heart that is my "wellspring of life" (Proverbs 4:23).

My heart was broken when I first learned of my daughter's decision, and it still is, as I write. Can I do any good in a broken state? No.

Ah, the miracle of hope. I trust. I believe. I slowly heal, although a part of me remains broken. I must live through each day, and with hope in my heart, I get stronger.

With God's hope I grow in understanding and wisdom. I don't understand everything, and don't like everything, but the confidence I have in God demands my trust as He works in my life. I can't imagine the turmoil my life would be in if the assurance of hope didn't rest in my heart.

Hope. A four-letter word that God gave us so we can wake up each morning and go on. That's what I'm doing.

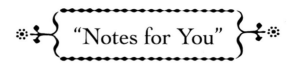

"Notes for You"

Many years ago I wrote the first verse from my favorite hymns on 3 x 5 index cards. On my drive to and from my job, I'd sing my way down the road. It was a refreshing time for me, and now I've become better acquainted with the words in each song. I'm thankful for the opportunity I've had to concentrate on the words of great hymns, as well as the joy I receive singing them. I know I don't make "beautiful music," but as Psalm 28:7b says: "My heart leaps for joy, and I will give thanks to Him in song."

Even now, twenty years later, I still sing my "Melody of Hymns." I don't remember every word as well as I'd like, but there's enough in my memory to keep me joyfully singing for thirty minutes.

I know God spoke to my inner ear and planted this idea in my mind. I was going through a difficult time on my job. Many mornings I cried driving down the road. I needed something to encourage me, and I thought of singing hymns.

Once I'd written the verses on cards, I started singing them every day in the same order. I didn't realize I would commit these songs to memory. But after four months I had a melody of hymns of my own.

This one exercise has done more for me than just getting me through a difficult time. At least once a week I sing my melody of hymns as I drive. I love the old hymns and recalling them at any time for my own personal little encouragement session is wonderful.

As I consider what happened from this experience, I wonder if I should write down a favorite psalm to repeat each day, as I did with these hymns, and commit it to memory. My first choice will be Psalm 103. I'll let you know how it turns out!

Cards Galore

What fun I have buying note cards and note paper! You can buy them everywhere, with every imaginable picture, in any size, and in different quantities. Having an abundance of cards and paper to choose from when I sit down to write a note brings me joy. It enhances my desire to write a note, and I always find just the right card or paper that conveys the thoughts I want to express.

Note cards have pictures on the front that give me a creative choice as to the tone of the message I wish to send. Some have encouraging words such as, "Hope your day is packed with specialness!" and "God's love enfolds us all." You can purchase ten cards starting as low as $2, envelopes included, in many places.

Note paper is another wonderful choice. Some have a verse of scripture and lightly engraved scenes, which make a pleasant background. Others convey tender scenes picturing animals and flowers. I have one tablet of paper decorated with bright lollipops, and I use this paper for "Congratulations" and "Thinking of You" notes. Tablets of paper start as low as $2, with 30 to 50 pages in each tablet. You will need to purchase envelopes for mailing.

Don't forget the value of a plain sheet of paper. Your message will arrive with the same warmth as if it had been written on the most attractive note paper. One of my most treasured notes was written on yellow tablet paper.

I have also received notes written on postcards. Postcards offer space for several sentences and are just as useful as a note card to convey encouraging words.Their message will not be private so you will need to write words that do not draw attention to a concern.

Vacation brings another opportunity to find different note cards and note paper. Many places you visit have specially sketched scenes of the surrounding area that you would not find elsewhere. This gives your reader a touch from a place they may not have visited.

More recently I've begun making my own cards from pictures I take. I'm an avid photographer and love to choose scenes that make me smile. With digital cameras and photography programs like Photoshop, you can make cards in a variety of ways. Also special are cards that are stamped with rubber-stamp art. I've received a number of handmade cards and the creativity is splendid!

There are many choices when picking out note cards and note paper to write on. The expense is minimal and a delightful touch can be added to your message. I keep many different cards and papers on hand so I'll have a good variety to choose from as I dwell on the words I'll be writing.

Remember, though, it's not the paper the receiver's eyes remember— your words will be the lasting memory.

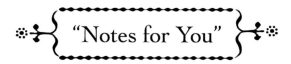

"Notes for You"

There's something special that happens when the calendar turns over to November. For the past several years, when November arrives, I think about those people who are or have been special in my life during that year. As God directs, I write a special note to each one, thanking them for the impact they've had on me. We never know how a note or letter we've written may have an everlasting impact on the receiver. What better time of the year than the month of Thanksgiving to share our hearts.

I call it "November Joy," and since beginning this practice I find my perspective regarding the coming Thanksgiving and Christmas season is one of contentment of heart. All my holiday planning runs smooth because I've already given my most important gifts of the Christmas season—gifts from my heart.

Different people impact my life each year. Mary is an example of a woman filled with God's love. Rachel displays Christ-like wisdom and knowledge. Penny has the gift of hospitality and shares joy. Carol demonstrates discernment and understanding. Jeanette has taught me the joy of going the extra mile for others.

Jerry is an example of unselfish love and a helping hand. Lee exhibits the woman of Titus 2 and Barbara encourages my heart as Onesiphorus did for Paul (2 Timothy 1:16). Elaine is a perfect example of a giving heart. Linda values our long-time friendship and that encourages me. Tom displays God's grace to others.

Everybody appreciates being thanked for something they have done. A simple "thank you" says: "I've noticed your kindness and it means something to me." This simple act will inspire the recipient and encourage them to continue using the gifts God instilled in them.

I need to tell people the difference they have made in my life. And I do!

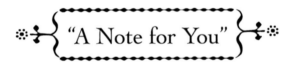

"A Note for You"

My dog, Emma, is the most relaxed dog I've ever known. She rolls on her back and lays with all four legs spread apart. She has no concern or worry about being attacked, even though she's so vulnerable in that position. I wish I could be that free from concern and worry. I must continue to have complete trust in Jesus, for I know He is my protector. Nothing can come my way except through His perfect will for me. My sweet Emma is a good example of displaying complete trust.

Emma certainly gives me joy. I have a magnet on my refrigerator door that says: "If your dog thinks you're the greatest, don't seek a second opinion." Emma thinks I'm great!

Animals are so much fun. They ask so little from us and give so much to us. I'm thankful God created animals for us to have as pets.

But I can't seem to be carefree like Emma. Concerns and worries are hard for me to deal with. When each new problem arises it takes me a while to completely turn it over to God.

There's just something about trying to figure out what's happening myself before I can let it go. Depending on how big the concern is, I can get myself in a lot of trouble before I'm begging God to handle it.

I think I'm getting better. My turnover time keeps getting shorter as the years go by. With each situation I conquer, I learn to trust even more.

Yes, Emma does help me. But only as a dog can. It's God who I must depend on.

A Worthy Service

I particularly enjoy the scripture that reads: "If you have any encouragement from being united with Christ, if any comfort from his love, if any fellowship with the Spirit, if any tenderness and compassion, then make my joy complete by being like-minded, having the same love, being one in spirit and purpose" (Philippians 2:1-2).

This verse inspires me to be faithful in the work God has gifted me to do.

Two gifts God tells us about in His Word are the ability to encourage, and showing mercy to others. Encouraging means to inspire with courage, spirit, or hope. Showing mercy means to have compassion for someone. Both of these gifts can be utilized through note writing.

My first experience with writing encouraging notes came before my birth into the Christian faith. There was a telephone message waiting for me one Monday morning where I was taking a training class. When I returned the call, a co-worker spoke words I didn't want to hear.

"Carol, Linda almost died. She has spinal meningitis." Patti spoke with me a little longer but I didn't hear what she said. The tears were spilling onto my cheeks.

Linda is my friend. A dear friend. We met at a time when I needed someone to accept me. Linda and her family took me in, and I became a part of their family.

Now it was Linda who needed me. I responded to her through notes and cards. I wanted her to know how much I was thinking of her.

The only way I knew how to always be there was through notes. She still recalls those notes I sent and they are a constant reminder of our friendship.

Linda is fine today. Many years have passed since her illness. But the benefits I received from the cards and notes I sent her are still with me. A seed was planted. I liked what I did. But it was many years later before I realized how important note writing is to the one on the receiving end. I cried when I received my first note and it made an immeasurable impression in my mind.

Note writing is a quiet ministry in God's kingdom. You may never receive attention for this service. Occasionally, you will receive an expression of gratitude from someone, or a new friendship will develop. Once, our pastor told Jerry and me that one couple had asked him if we had been assigned to encourage them. We were so attentive they couldn't believe anyone would just reach out as we did.

If your heart is prepared by God for note writing you will not depend on the responses you receive to continue doing it. Each note you write will bring joy to your heart. You couldn't stop if you wanted to. But over the course of time, responses do come. I have a treasure box where I put special notes sent to me.

The world cries out for caring people, a warm heart, an encouraging word. Note writing, a worthy service to your fellow sojourner, is the perfect answer.

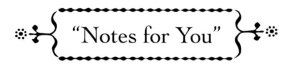

"Notes for You"

Recently my pastor read a literal translation of Proverbs 4:23, which reads: "Above all else, guard your heart, for it is the wellspring of life." The translation I heard says: "More than all else to be watched over and protected (as something in a confined place) it is imperative that you preserve and keep your heart sensitive; because from within it comes divine direction for your life." I've always loved this verse, believing it had great significance in my life. I know Jesus wants my heart to be filled with joy. How can it be done? By keeping my eye on Him!

My heart has taken two or three severe wounds because of the hurricanes I've gone through. These wounds are imbedded in my very being and have changed the course of my life completely. Because of memory, wounds can't completely heal. But I can repair them and continue with life. The above verse urges me to care for my heart.

The "wellspring of life." With no heart, there's no life. Whether my heart is strong or damaged, with the right medicine I can continue on each day.

The medicine I take is exposing myself to good and right things. Philippians 4:8 tells us: "Whatever is true, whatever is noble, whatever is right, whatever is pure, whatever is lovely, whatever is admirable—if anything is excellent or praiseworthy—think about such things."

This is what I want to do.

When I expose myself to questionable or hurtful things, I send unhealthy images to my mind. Thoughts prompted by those images weaken my mind, causing it to become vulnerable to impure thoughts.

Taking care of my heart with good medicine supplies me with a healthy life—both inside and outside.

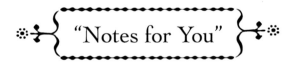

"Notes for You"

I attended a conference last weekend and during the worship service each person was given "sealed orders" and sent away for twenty minutes of individual meditation. Psalm 8 was our text of study and during our quiet time with God we were instructed to answer some questions regarding God's creation and the details of His work. I was reminded that God thinks I'm special and made me just the way I am. I hope today you know and appreciate how special you are to God.

It doesn't take much for me to put myself down. I'm armed with a ready recital of all my faults and problems. My self-image has never been great and is the cause of many of my failures.

But God says He made me just the way I am. He knows everything about me—all my rough edges, my weaknesses, and that lowly self-image I carry around—and He still loves me!

It's God desire and will for me to be a better person through my relationship with Jesus. He can overcome my weaknesses and teach me in areas that are problems for me. He's done just that with my insecurity and shyness, allowing me to write encouraging notes.

And He's adjusted my attitude and outlook in general and improved my perception of life. Thankfully, He isn't finished with me yet. Imagine, I am His design and He cares for me!

The words of Psalm 8 are lovely: *"O Lord, our Lord, how majestic is your name in all the earth! You have set your glory above the heavens. From the lips of children and infants you have ordained praise because of your enemies, to silence the foe and the avenger. When I consider your heavens, the work of your fingers, the moon and the stars, which you have set in place, what is man that you are mindful of him, the son of man that you care for him? You made him a little lower than the heavenly beings and crowned him with glory and honor. You made him ruler over the works of your hands; you put everything under his feet: all flocks and herds, and the beasts of the field, the birds of the air, and the fish of the sea, all that swim the paths of the seas. O Lord, our Lord, how majestic is your name in all the earth!"*

Go for It!

Let me take you back several years and share portions of a poem I wrote. "Baked with Love" tells the story of a chocolate chip coffee cake I baked for a good friend.

> "I go all together with flour and sugar,
> Some mixing and stirring, some soda and water,
> But my magic is added and oh can you tell,
> That I'm meant for someone who's sure thought of well."

That was one of my first stabs at creative writing. Reading those four lines, you can understand why I didn't include the entire poem for you to read!

Writing a poem about a chocolate chip coffee cake? How silly! But it wasn't a silly idea to me. I wanted to add a special touch to my home-baked gift. And much to the chagrin of several close friends, there were many more poems through the years.

What does this have to do with writing notes? It was my beginning in writing and a beginning is necessary for anything you do. After I exhausted my efforts at writing poems, I began writing articles. Articles brought stories, and then God's grace brought notes.

Of all the phases I ventured into, none captured my heart as much as simple note writing. Perhaps it is the intimate sharing with just one other person. My note will only be shared between me and the receiver. Or it may be the anticipation of seeing that person with a smile on their face—especially if they are going through a difficult time.

It's not that I'm the greatest note writer. My words are simply from the heart. Having a positive impact in someone's life brings enormous satisfaction and is a great motivator for me to write. Writing notes has brought me more enjoyment than any other writing project.

In some situations there just isn't much anyone can do. Yet, a note that simply says "I care about you" says what a million words never could. My words are honest. If I write that I've prayed for someone, it's because I have.

Are you wondering if you can write an encouraging note? You may be thinking, "Not me!" But whether you've dabbled in any form of writing, or you're a novice, note writing *is* within your reach. I believe you *can* write a note of encouragement.

Let's begin. Is your imagination piqued with the thought, "Can I really do it?" Aside from a little confidence to plunge ahead, and readable penmanship, there is virtually no skill needed to sit down and write a note.

There's no editing to be scrutinized by a professional; no sentence structure to worry about. No English teacher will be looking over your shoulder, telling you, "Your subordinate clause is incorrect." Notes are quick to complete and in the mail before you know it.

Don't waste another moment. I'm excited for you! As you share yourself with others, you will find a special fulfillment in understanding and caring about them. You can do it. All it takes is a beginning.

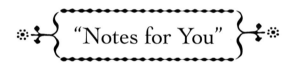

"Notes for You"

I attended a party today for my grandmother's 90th birthday. An event such as this causes one to consider the future. To my surprise, I thought of this verse from Proverbs: "Gray hair is a crown of splendor; it is attained by a righteous life" (16:31). I've found as my own hair fills in with the "sparkle" of gray, I want it to be from righteous living. Most of the time I fail miserably, but the desire is in my heart. God knows our hearts and works in us accordingly. Our future will bring gray hairs, yet we can smile at them, too, for God saw fit to include them in His Holy Word.

I find it amazing that God put gray hair in His Word. Gray hair is not desired in our society, and many people try and wash the gray away. I've never been concerned about my gray hair. When I first discovered God's opinion of gray hair in Scripture, I was quite pleased.

Regarding this verse, Matthew Henry's *Concise Commentary* says "Old people especially should be found in the way of religion and godliness." I have several friends that are many years older than me. The thing I enjoy about them the most is the wisdom and understanding they demonstrate. Jeanne is one of those people.

I sat next to Jeanne in the choir loft at my home church and we took to one another right away. She saw a single mother who needed support and encouragement, and I saw a gracious woman who accepted me. Many pearls of wisdom were received from Jeanne as I dealt with my prodigal daughter. Jeanne carried her age well from many years of trusting God with the concerns of life.

When I'm older and completely gray, I hope my hair will represent righteous living. I'm certainly working on it.

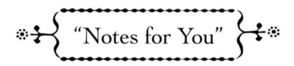

"Notes for You"

I recently listened to a CD tape by Joyce Landorf-Heatherley titled: "Balcony People." She talks about those people who cheer you on and encourage you through life. I know I need balcony people in my life. And I hope I'm a balcony person to people I know. We all need support from people who care about us.

One of my balcony people is Pam. She was a co-worker many years ago. We found we had similar interests and became friends. I was in the beginning stages of writing when we met. I needed someone to critique my work and offer suggestions.

As Pam had a side interest in writing, she agreed to critique my work. And since that time Pam continually encourages me in my writing as I create new projects. She went with me to my first writers' conference and showed interest and support for the dreams I have. Pam willingly spends time to help me in this work. Pam is a true balcony person.

Carol is another of my balcony people. I work with Carol, and again, similar interests drew us together.

Carol has the gift of discernment. She listens to things I tell her and guides me in determining my best course of action. I can depend on her understanding of a situation as she helps me see godly understanding. A Christian since childhood, her wisdom helps this "younger" Christian as I walk down the path God has put me on.

Pam and Carol are two of my balcony people. I'm so glad!

Situations of Life

That Awful Cold

From a simple cold to major surgery, a day is more pleasant when you receive a note. Although a note will not relieve the symptoms, it does bring a bright spot to an otherwise uncomfortable day. It's an excellent way to divert someone's attention from his or her problems to other thoughts.

We can all relate to the discomfort and aggravation of a cold or flu. It always arrives at the most inopportune time and four or five days pass before we're on our feet again. A simple expression of cheer will do wonders to promote a smile.

When someone is confined to a hospital or their home for several months, constant reassurance that you miss them will ease the recovery process. It's easy for the patient to think nobody cares. The waiting becomes more difficult as time passes. Your note tells them you care.

In a more serious illness, where recovery is not certain, words are indeed hard to come by. In my notes, I express a daily need to trust God and look to Him for comfort and rest. When you send a note each week to remind someone that God loves them and is with them every moment of the day, it helps them to focus on their faith ... the only thing that will get them through.

Write about the joy of God's creation—the flowers and trees, the sun and stars—nature is a good spirit booster. Every spring, when the maple tree outside my window brings forth baby leaves, they always find their way into a few notes. It's God's way of showing me there is hope.

Bringing someone's thoughts in line to God's control over the universe helps them to see He has control over them, too.

Whether it's a serious illness or a passing flu, you have the ability to brighten someone's day!

* * * * * * * * *

"I hope this cheerful note, filled with love, brings a smile to your face and joy to your heart. I know God is watching over you, and I'm thankful we have a God we can trust with all of our heart's concerns."

"Just a note to let you know you are missed. I hope you are doing well and your heart is filled with the peace and joy Jesus has just for you. In all the concerns and decisions in your life, trust Jesus to guide and direct you, for He is the only one who can give you perfect peace."

"As you prepare for your operation, may you know God is hearing prayers from many friends and loved ones for His care over you. You can trust Him to be your constant companion."

"I am thankful your operation is over and you are resting at home. May the warmth of your home comfort you and help you relax. Jesus is right beside you, helping you every step of the way."

"Although I can't be with you right now, know my thoughts and prayers are with you. It will be difficult for awhile, but soon God will restore you and your days will be active once again."

"May each day become brighter for you as you trust Jesus during this time. And may joy be in your heart, knowing your brothers and sisters are praying for you, lifting your concern to our Father."

"I'm sorry to hear that the tumor was malignant, but rejoice that they were able to get it all. With the treatment you receive, you'll be a new and remodeled version of the [person's name] we love."

"You are being supported by the prayers of God's people. How wonderful to know He hears! What a great God we have. May His healing and comfort continually touch your body and soul. May your health be restored quickly. I care."

"It must be difficult, and scary, as you seek the best course of action for treatment. May your heart be assured that God will be with you each step of the way. He will refresh your soul. Our God is the God of HOPE! How thankful I am."

"We never know when our life will be changed by an illness, but we always know God is with us. He's with you right now, sending His love through this simple note. And He'll be with you in every decision you make. Let Him lead you beside still and quiet waters, where He will give rest to your soul and hope to your heart."

"The changing of the seasons—always a beautiful display of God's creation. Change must be good since this is the way God made the earth. Yet, I am glad, and thankful, that one thing doesn't change— God's love for us! I'm praying that the God of miracles overwhelms you with His incredible goodness as you trust Him with the care of your eyes."

"Rest in God's everlasting arms, and use this time of healing as a special time to be with Him, letting Him be your courage and strength. May you find special refreshment this week knowing He cares for you."

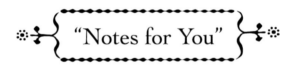

"Notes for You"

Our God gives us wonderful promises to help us each day—they are promises we can trust. What a joy to know our Lord loves and cares for us and we can share that joy with others. One promise that always comforts my heart is found in John 14:2-3: "I am going there to prepare a place for you." What a promise! These words soothe my soul. Living on this earth has its hard times. Knowing that Jesus is preparing a place for me makes it easier for me to keep moving forward.

The rest of that passage of scripture reads: "In my Father's house are many rooms; if it were not so, I would have told you. I am going there to prepare a place for you. And if I go and prepare a place for you, I will come back and take you to be with me that you also may be where I am."

God's Word is full of wonderful promises. His promises get me through anything that comes into my life. I have held tight to many of His strong words as I faced difficulty and hurt. Here are some of my favorites:

2 Timothy 1:7, "For God did not give us a spirit of timidity, but a spirit of power, of love and of self-discipline." I confess, fear and timidity have plagued me through most of my life. This is one verse in Scripture that helps me overcome my weakness and spread my wings.

James 1:12, "Blessed is the man who perseveres under trial, because when he has stood the test, he will receive the crown of life that God has promised to those who love him." This verse has been a lifeline during many trials. Persevere under trial. That's hard. But with God's love I'm able to do just that.

1 John 4:4b, "The one who is in you is greater than the one who is in the world." Knowing there is one greater than Satan helps me deal with the times I'm anxious. One day Jesus will return to this earth and reign—He's going to win!

All doubt is gone when we hear His Word and believe it. They are the truest words we will ever hear. And that calls for joy!

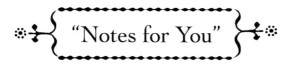
"Notes for You"

"I'm thinking of you today. I pray the Lord will be with you in a special way, filling your life with SONshine, overflowing with cheer. Above every cloud in the sky—grey or fluffy white—He shines bright and warms us with His light. God bless you today."

The first time I flew in an airplane, I experienced a wonderful discovery. The sun always shines!

I was traveling home after visiting my sister who lives in another state. The storm clouds in the sky were dark and dreary. When the plane took off, up, up, up we climbed until all at once we reached the other side of the clouds. My eyes were blinded by the brightness of the sun and the stunning blue sky. The sun was shining!

I went from a dark, gloomy perception to a hopeful, promising new impression. I've never forgotten the feeling I received that day coming out of the clouds. My heart smiled. Security calmed my fears. I was reminded that God is always with us.

When I can't see the sun, it's easy to forget that it still shines. Whether the sun is hidden behind storm clouds or behind clouds of my own making, things can look very bleak. Because of my experience while flying, I know God's love shines bright, even if I can't see it.

We can always have SONshine in our hearts because He is always with us. A day can be special if we only remember God is above every cloud.

Comforting the Grieving

There are few words that can give real comfort to someone who has lost a loved one. Different emotions surface in all of us when we lose someone close to us. When I come face-to-face with a person who is grieving, I reach for their hand and share a hug with them. But when it comes to words … my mind too often draws a blank.

When I've learned of someone's death, I first send a card to the grieving friend or family. There are many varieties of cards to choose from. In a few days, though, I write a note, sharing from my heart.

If I personally knew the person who died, I express how special they were to me. Expressing my true feelings identifies with the grieving person. Through my sharing, the grieved person may reach out to me for comfort. If I didn't know the person who died, I share my sympathy just by saying "I care … my thoughts and prayers are with you."

I don't stop there. In two or three weeks, I write another note, reminding them I'm thinking about them, and praying for them during their time of grief. Then, over the next several months, I continue to remember them with notes filled with caring words. This small effort on my part produces an array of positive feelings to help the other person work through their loss.

All members of a family need to be remembered. A child who loses a father; a husband who loses a wife; a father who loses a son, and a friend who loses a special person—they all need reminders of God's love in their time of loss.

The simplest words are the best words to write. Sharing those words is what counts. Do it!

★ ★ ★ ★ ★ ★ ★ ★

"My friend, I was saddened to hear of your loss. My prayers are with you each day. May God bring you comfort at this time."

"I just heard about your loss and my heart is sad. May your tears help relieve your grief, and may God's comfort come to you in a special way as others share in your sorrow."

"You are in my heart. Each day I ask God to bless you with His strength. Through the promises of Jesus, we can trust Him to work and bring His wonderful comfort to us. I love you."

"I hurt as we grieve over [person's name] death. He was a very special friend to us. It will be difficult not having him near us. I know God is close to us right now."

"Your life may be difficult and confusing right now. As you begin each new day, Jesus is beside you and desires to help you. Believe in Him to bring rest to your heart."

"In this new week, I hope there is joy in your heart, knowing God is Almighty. Only through Him do we receive the deep comfort and peace to sustain us through difficult times. You are very special to Him and to me."

"I just want to send some joy to you today as you continue to trust Jesus with all your needs. He is able to overcome all our heartaches and it's wonderful to trust Him."

"In our sorrow we may not feel His presence, but that doesn't change His promise to be with us. I pray God will ease your heart and surround you with His love."

"It is so special that we have a Lord and Savior who has walked the valleys of life as well as the mountaintops. It is my prayer that His abiding presence, His infinite wisdom, and His eternal purpose will be very real to you, and a source of strength and abiding hope."

"The Lord provides so many good things in our lives that we might think He's abandoned us when sorrow comes along. But the Lord knows when we're hurting and it's then that He draws closer to us."

"We must never give up on our hope, for it is alive, and we can trust that it will carry us through all things. God will continue to provide the courage you need. I just want you to know you're covered by God's love and my prayers."

"I send my sympathy to you in the death of your father, and hope God's presence in your heart is helping you each day. He is the great Comforter, and He's always with you."

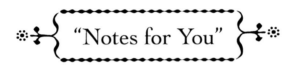

"Notes for You"

One of my favorite devotional books is "Streams in the Desert" by Mrs. Charles E. Cowman. In volume 1, from the August 28 devotion where Mrs. Cowman quotes John Macduff, this sentence caught my eye: "Oh, happy are we if the hurricanes that ripple life's unquiet sea have the effect of making Jesus more precious." Although no storm is ever wanted or desired, God says He will go through it with us. And as we lean on Jesus, trusting Him, we learn more about Him. He becomes more precious to us. I'm glad we share Jesus and can rejoice together in God's wonderful gift to us.

The hurricanes of life—I really dislike them. They hit deep in the core of my being and it's a challenge to continue each day. But thoughts like the one above sure help me get through them.

One of my biggest storms was divorce. It shook me and threw me, leaving me in a state of disaster and despair. When the storm ended, I was at the bottom of life's pit.

But I had the book. The book to guide me safely to rest. God's Word— the Bible. And that sentence I quoted above is true. Jesus became more precious.

I've found that storms can bring something good when you seek God's help. From the storm of divorce I discovered my life's area of service—note writing. At a pivotal point of need someone sent a note to encourage me; someone I didn't know personally. That one note changed my life. Someone cared.

Streams in the Desert points you to the one who heals and restores your soul. It helps you see your hurricane through the eyes of faith. It's a good accessory to God's Word and helps you see trials in a new light so that your spirit is calmed and you make it through the storm.

With the one who controls hurricanes at your side, you won't get blown away!

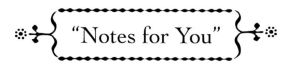

"Notes for You"

This weekend my sister, Kathy, and her husband are visiting from Oklahoma. It's been four and a half years since I've seen my sister. I was reflecting on how different my life would have been if she lived close to me. But there are other "sisters" living close to me—my sisters in Christ. They have affected my life in wondrous ways. I'm thankful for them.

There have been many "sisters" for me to enjoy and share life with. And I love them just as I do my blood sister.

I remember Clara, some fifteen years my senior, who I met when I was a new believer. We both had come to a new Sunday school class for older single adults, and over the course of a few weeks we became friends.

Clara became my big sister here at home. We talked on the phone and went to fellowship events together. We were both quiet individuals and subdued in a group, but we worked well together.

Clara was my first sister in Christ. Her faith was mature, as she had come to belief in Christ many years before me. Her example of a godly woman helped shape my life to reflect God's love.

Through all those years, as Clara helped me when I walked through difficult situations, I never dreamed an opportunity would arise for me to help her. But as years passed, the calm assurance she shared with me I now return to her in similar support.

The relationships I develop with my sisters in Christ play an important part in my life. Kathy still lives far away. We enjoy each other through telephone calls and e-mail. But I'll always remember Clara and the impact her walk with Christ made on me as a new believer.

Shining Affirmation

"I'm sending you this note to tell you God loves you, and I think you're special too." WOW! How does that make you feel? If you're anything like me, your self-esteem shot sky high.

What joy a simple statement can bring. Why do we find it so hard to express thoughts that expose our feelings? We have all that is necessary to encourage someone and so often we keep it to ourselves.

Occasionally I'll remember people who helped me through difficult times. The support they gave me is engraved on my heart. When I remember them, I take the time to send them a note, and thank them for all they did for me.

Is there someone you haven't seen in awhile that you'd like to touch base with? It's so easy to do nothing and let the opportunity pass. But your note may come at just the time when that person needs encouraging.

My friend's daughter, Mary, is an avid basketball player. Each year I watch her development with excitement. During each season her skill grows sharper and her potential increases.

At the end of basketball season I wrote a thank-you note to Mary's coach to express my appreciation for her ability and her desire to work with young people. Besides surprising her with affirmation unexpectedly, I hope she was encouraged to continue her work with even more enthusiasm.

People want to be appreciated and recognized for their skills and abilities. I know there must be people you appreciate and remember with fond thoughts. Too little is done for people who are making a difference in our world. You never know what is happening in another's life. If God brings someone to your mind, it's a perfect opportunity to remember them with a note.

* * * * * * * * *

"I'm writing you this note so you will know you are special to Jesus and to me. I enjoy your smile when I see you … it always makes me feel better when I am down."

"Thank you for sharing your gift of organ playing with us. You played one of my favorite songs on Sunday and it sounded beautiful. I appreciate that you give your time and talent each Sunday morning to worship God and bring us joy."

"This is a special thank-you for the love and concern God has given you for others, and for your teaching ability that Jerry and I so enjoy. May God continue to use you to teach His Word and encourage those He's placed in your care."

"Congratulations on another fine year as Wheaton's drama teacher. Of the two years Elisabeth has sat under your teaching, I am thankful she had a coach that displayed a calm assurance and a good-tempered composure while instructing the students. Thank you for your dedication."

"I'm sending this note to say hello and let you know you are in my thoughts. I hope the transition to your new church has been comforting and that God has eased the hurt in your heart. It is wonderful to know He takes care of us, in His perfect way, through all of our life."

"Thank you for listening to God's voice and calling me yesterday. I felt so much better after talking with you. I know you understood how I was feeling, and sharing it with you helped me a lot. Our God is very good to us."

"Your sensitivity and warmth have blessed me. I'm grateful the Lord allowed our hearts to blend into friendship. I hope today you sense His love—and mine, too."

"I have been blessed by your giftedness, your vision, and your insight. May His calm and gentle presence bless you in abundance!"

"You are appreciated and loved for all you do for Christ and for the body of believers under your care. Thank you."

"I want you to know how much I've enjoyed studying the two 'mystery women' these last two weeks. Thanks for the time and effort you've spent preparing these lessons, as well as our studies throughout the year. God has opened a door for you in a new, but familiar area of work. I know you will be a blessing to the staff you will be working with, and I hope you'll find satisfaction and enjoyment in your new job."

"What a lovely and meaningful song you and your friends sang during worship Sunday morning. Your voices harmonized beautifully and it was a joy to hear you sing. I hope you will continue to use your gift of song to praise God."

"During these last years of Iola's life, you've given of yourself completely to care for her. In a note she wrote me, she said, 'Mary Jo is beyond anything I could ever imagine with her care.' This typifies the Christ-like spirit which is very evident in you. May the Lord continue to make you fruitful and encourage you in all your work for Him."

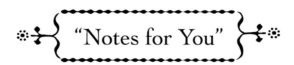

"Notes for You"

A few months ago I read an article about a lady who turned fifty. In celebration of this momentous occasion, she created a list of fifty reasons why she was thankful. I liked the idea and decided to make my own list. I'm now at number forty-six and it's been quite a project. Perhaps my fiftieth reason should be: "I'm glad I've created this list!" It's helped me to see the things that are most important in my life.

The list hangs on my writing room wall. Typed and laminated, it reminds me daily of the people and things I'm most thankful for. The creation of chocolate and potato chips made that list!

At about the same time I created my list, I created another list: "For Carol to be successful in life through my relationship with Jesus Christ, I must:" This list required an earnest understanding of what I believe God called me to do—encourage through note writing—and the best way for me to do it.

These are some of the things I must do or accept in order to accomplish His purpose in my life: I must accept that I'm a deep feeling and emotional person, a quality that enables me to empathize with others; I must spend time with God to prepare my heart; I need the solitude and the quiet of my home to work this ministry; I must not be distracted by self-doubt. Only I can accomplish God's purpose for my life, and it is good in His sight.

Both of my lists give me joy. One reminds me of all the people and things that make me happy. The other gives me direction on how to realize my greatest accomplishment during my time here on earth. Now, if I can just have my Mom's longevity and determination I'll be just fine!

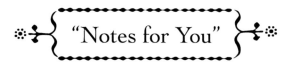

"Notes for You"

God has such special ways of bringing joy to all our days. This past week I've enjoyed fluffy white, cheerful clouds sailing against the blue sky; a downy woodpecker eating suet tied to our maple tree; a herd of deer running across the field—simple things, all special things that God created. May the Lord be with you in a special way this day!

Simplicity. Do you appreciate simple things? Do you slow down often to see the creation God has given us? I do.

I take country roads on my drive to my job each day so I can enjoy the scenery and separate myself from rush-hour madness. It takes me about fifteen minutes longer than if I take the highway, but the serenity it brings to my mind is well worth the extra time.

There are places I love to see when I drive. The meadow where wild flowers grow; the porch with the American flag hanging from the railing; the field where deer frequent—so many scenes I delight in each day. Each season of the year provides a different picture for me to enjoy.

When the weather permits, I spend many of my evenings sitting in my backyard for an hour, listening to the sounds of nature. That's also where Jerry and I catch many of the cloud formations that delight our eyes. It's a great way to spend an hour.

Simplicity. It's a hard choice. Our world beckons us to do and see everything or surely we will miss out on life. But I neither see everything nor do everything. I am seeing what's most important for my life—the ability to enjoy simple things and be satisfied.

Time is life, and I want to enjoy it's simplicity.

In the Family

All around us people are experiencing trials of life. I have never met a family that is exempt from the tragedies that find their way into our homes.

Some problems are easily perceived, such as the death of a family member, or an illness; others, such as the loss of a job, or dealing with a wayward child, are not quite as easy to detect. Keeping your ears alert to what people say can help you discern a need.

It is hard to admit to others that there are difficulties in our families. Embarrassment causes a person to shelter a problem. Telling others that a spouse or child is an alcoholic, or that an unwed young woman is pregnant, can be a humbling, even humiliating experience. That's why it is essential that the note writer have an awareness of what is going on around them. Whether we know what the situation is, or only that one exists, our response of caring is needed.

When we understand the importance of trusting Jesus through trials, we can greatly encourage others. People are hurting. Be prepared and willing to offer what God has taught you.

★ ★ ★ ★ ★ ★ ★ ★

"Many prayers are being spoken for you and your family during this difficult time. Remember that Jesus is right there with you to comfort and love you. I hope this day brings sunshine to your heart."

"Tears are one of the wonderful ways God has given us to relieve the concerns of our heart. I hope your heart is filled with His peace as you call upon Him for your every need."

51

"Sometimes God sends a signal out to others to let them know someone needs encouraging. So I'm sending you this little note to tell you I care about you, and I'm praying that God will give you direction and guidance."

"It is hard to sit back and watch as a loved one makes mistakes. I have shed many tears talking with Jesus, as I know you have also. As we pray for Him to work in [person's name] life, may He bring you peace and rest to trust Him with [his or her] life."

"Our God gives us wonderful promises to help us each day, and they are promises we can trust. What a joy to know our Lord loves and cares for us and we can share that joy with others."

"You are in my heart as you trust God to work in your family. He understands your worry and knows your concerns. He can bring peace to your heart … trust Him today."

"Friends are our special families in difficult times. Know that my heart holds you close. God's ways are perfect—His love is constant, and He is always, always faithful."

"There is no logical answer that our hearts can see, but we know there is a grace answer—an eternal answer. I pray God will ease your heart and pave a way for you to accept His will."

"You're in my heart and prayers, and I wish I could be there with you. But I trust God as your protector and strength, and know He will provide the courage you need to see you through. May you find rest under the shadow of His wings where nothing can harm you."

"When God goes through a difficult situation with us, He somehow strengthens and builds us supernaturally so that we can get through the trial at hand. Be encouraged, for His ear hears every prayer, and His hands hold you tight as He cares for you."

"It is good to know that someone lifts your name to God … that God hears your name because it comes through Jesus … that your name is with God. I hope your heart is encouraged knowing you are prayed for by your friends and loved ones. May you feel His touch and see His goodness today and every day."

"In the darkest moments of my life, I am learning God is most with me, and I learn more about who He is and how to really trust Him in all circumstances. I'm sure the next few weeks will be hard, but He will be there beside you. Just call out His name."

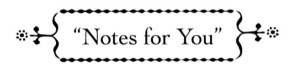

"Notes for You"

I watched my dog, Emma, soak up the afternoon sun as she relaxed on the hot blacktop driveway, just huffing and puffing away. I wanted to tell her: "If you'd get in the shade, it would be cooler." I know God says that to me when I'm huffing and puffing: "If you'd get in the shade and be refreshed by My Word, you'll feel a lot better." God's breath would flow through me and calm my soul.

If I don't stay consistent in my time with God, I feel the consequences: short-tempered, uninspired, and an unkind attitude. I also get mad at myself for getting away from my routine.

That's why I try and live my life based on discipline. I don't want to get out of the shade!

Discipline is good mental exercise and helps mold my willpower and self-control. Routine makes it easy to stay in a pattern each day and do what I have planned.

Discipline and routine go hand-in-hand. The routine of life could turn mundane unless the things I have determined to do are in my best mental, emotional, physical, and spiritual interest.

In his book "Lightposts for Living," Thomas Kinkade agrees about the need for routine in your life: "But I learned long ago that I need routine in my life—and that I have more freedom when my days can rely on a predictable rhythm ... Such repeated and dependable activities anchor my days, providing a sense of stability."

I know that staying in God's Word is one thing that helps me go through each day. It keeps me balanced and in tune to the right way. I want to do all I can to make that a part of my day. Then I am refreshed and have the energy to do the things that come my way.

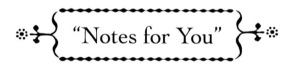

"Notes for You"

In the pastor's office at my home church there is a large sign that runs across one wall. It reads: "Keep Your Eye on the Goal." Our pastor has referred to this sign often, and it comes to my mind often, too. No matter what happens from day to day, as long as I "keep my eye on the goal"—Jesus—everything will be okay.

So many things happen during the course of a day that it's very easy for me to lose sight of what's important. My pastor's sign reminds me the goal is Jesus.

I had an especially difficult time when I accepted a job in a church office. I discovered that working in a Christian environment can be just as stressful as any other office. People are people. We all make mistakes, get angry, and act in ways we shouldn't.

Even so, I was astounded that I faced the same difficulties that I faced in a secular work environment. It became very easy for me to get worked up over non-Christian behavior by my co-workers. It didn't take long for my behavior to get out of line, too.

I discovered I have a tendency to be "short" with people I talk with on the phone. An ugly lack of patience on my part. This practice continued until I couldn't stand it anymore—it was unacceptable to me. I had to face my sin.

After a little talk with God and my request for Him to change me, I was quite conscious of my conversation when talking on the phone. "Remember, Carol, don't be short" would flow through my mind.

Keep my eye on the goal!

Family Breakup

From my experience, people tend to step away from individuals who are dealing with separation or divorce. They don't want to get involved so they keep their distance. My advice is: those going through separation or divorce need your encouragement … greatly!

Separated and divorced individuals need your encouragement and care just as much as someone who has lost a spouse through death. They experience a total spectrum of negative feelings. They may also deal with embarrassment as they interact with their church family.

The dreams of separated and divorced people are shattered. A marriage relationship, when broken, destroys self-esteem. Humility is lived within every day.

Advice is not appropriate. Let them know you care about them and are praying for them. Provide words that will lead them to seek Jesus; words that will turn them to Him for guidance.

Share their hurt, encouraging them to go on. There is life after divorce. Because of God's grace, often life will be far greater than what they experienced before. A broken person, when rebuilt by God, is a strong servant. Often, their ability to comfort others surpasses fellow believers who offer comfort because of the lessons God has taught them.

Very few people reach out to those experiencing separation and divorce. Don't hesitate to write a note of encouragement. Take care in the words you write. Be sure that they only comfort with God's love and help build the self-esteem of the receiver.

★ ★ ★ ★ ★ ★ ★ ★ ★

"It's a difficult time for you right now, of not understanding and hurting inside. Trust completely in God as He guides and comforts you. He is able to bring peace to your heart and light your way each day."

"I care about you, knowing your life is hard right now. Keep very close to Jesus, even though your heart is breaking. I understand what you're going through because I've been there. You can depend on Him each step of the way."

"I have you in my heart and pray for you as God shows you His will. Trust Him with everything; He will protect your heart and guide you in the right direction. And remember how special you are to Jesus."

"It is good to see, when everything is not quite right, that you can go on and serve God. We appreciate you leading the singing on Sunday morning, in your father's absence, especially with your heart struggling with concern. Our God is faithful and loves you very much."

"You are in my heart and prayers at this time, and I hope you feel the love being sent your way. I trust God's wonderful promises are bringing you comfort and the assurance that He is working. May His love bring you joy."

"God is faithful, and He's with you right now to comfort and care for you. How wonderful it is to be held in His arms and know He is in control. His ways are greater than we could ever imagine, and I know He is working in your life. Trust Him."

"My prayer is that our Lord's presence, strength, and peace will be very real to you today. Take each day one at a time. He accompanies us through every hour and is there each minute. We don't have to go it alone."

"Last week is behind you and God has given you a new week with his love and promises. Trust Him as you go through each day. I pray for you and believe God will calm your heart and help you to understand His will. I'm so thankful we can trust Him with all our needs."

"I'm so glad our God is the God of second chances, and 3rd and 4th, and as many retries as we need, as long as we keep our focus on Him, and keep trying. You will soon get into a routine rhythm, and feel more comfortable with your obligations. Although things don't always go as we want, God doesn't give up on us, and for that we can be truly thankful!"

"God doesn't want you to be lonely. That's why He's called us together in His church, so we can be part of His family. But even then, if we don't make the effort to be involved, we can still be lonely. You have a demanding schedule to be here, there, and everywhere, but you still need to find the time to take part in activities so you can feel a part of the family. Even if you can't attend all of an activity, being there for any amount of time will be beneficial. God loves you, and He wants you to be happy and have joy in your heart."

"We are so fortunate to be in Jesus' hands. What a great encouragement it is to know that we are never alone, and God is always working in our lives. May your heart be refreshed as you ponder this good news."

"Keep believing and trusting, and calling to God. No matter what happens day to day, God continues to work. The dawn of a new day brings His promise to be with us. That's a joy we can smile about! I'm sure the adjustment of living alone is still difficult. My heart is with you."

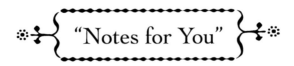

"Notes for You"

I received a card from a dear friend this week and it reminded me of the blessings of friendship. Linda and I go back to junior high school days, and although distance separates us and months may pass between communications, the bond is strong and good. This special contact from her helps me remember other friends who are far from my door but near to my heart.

Friends are very important to me. I make every effort to maintain the friendships God has brought my way. I have friends from every period of my life.

Maintaining a friendship means I make contact with my friends in a timely manner. For friends who live far away, that may mean writing or calling them three or four times a year. For those friends who live near me, it means contacting them every other month and meeting them for fellowship.

The most important thing I can do for my friends is pray for them. If I don't have any contact with them, my prayers would be aimless and general. By keeping in touch with my friends, my prayers can be specific and current.

The bond that is built with a friend can bring trust and joy to a relationship. All uneasiness disappears when I need help because I have confidence and reassurance from people who care about me.

Anne is one of those people. We worked together many years ago, and before she moved south we would meet each year for dinner. Our faith sealed our friendship. Anne was always there for me and was one of the first people to share in my happiness when Jerry and I married. I know I can call Anne at any time and she will be available to help me.

You must be a friend to have a friend. I need the support that friends give me. Thank you, Anne, for being my friend.

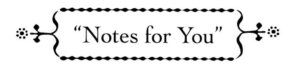

"Notes for You"

It sure has been hot lately! It makes it hard to get excited about doing anything. But God's Word is refreshing; it cools our heart. His words provide the cool touch we need to refresh our bodies and calm our spirit. I hope you enjoy His Word today.

I love to read God's Word. A number of years ago I decided to read the Bible from beginning to end. I had never done it before.

Reading the Bible from beginning to end seemed like an impossible project. To put this undertaking within my reach, I decided there would be no timetable to distract me. I made up my mind to accomplish this goal in a steady manner.

I read one chapter in the Bible and the same chapter in a commentary. Then I moved on to the next chapter. This helped me understand what I read and gave proper meaning to each chapter.

It took me two years to go through the entire Bible. I proceeded in a well-ordered state of mind, choosing to enjoy the adventure instead of accomplishing a goal. It was one of the most rewarding things I've ever done.

I didn't learn a lot as far as content because the teaching I received from my home church, when I was a new Christian, was excellent. I knew a lot of the Bible before I began. What I did receive was clarity—God's story was clearer. My grasp of the Scriptures as a total picture became focused.

Yes, it was refreshing! So refreshing that's it's time to start again.

Good News

There are special times in our lives when a personal achievement is realized or an important occasion takes place. It's a time of sharing good news with friends and loved ones. These are joyous occasions.

Weddings are one of those times. Cards and gifts are always appropriate, but try something different. I think about the nervousness that usually settles in on a couple before the wedding day and write a note to reassure them of God's guidance in the decisions they are making. Letting a couple know you are interested in their welfare is an open door to communication, if a need exists.

The birth of a baby is another special occasion. A proud new mother and father will love the extra attention they receive from a short note wishing them well. Receiving encouragement a few weeks after the baby is born (and sleepless nights have taken over!) will be welcome support as they care for their child.

Your friend finally received a long-awaited promotion in his or her chosen field. There will be change as he or she pursues the challenges of the new job. Encourage them! Express your happiness for their success. They deserve a pat on the back for their hard work.

Remembering a young person as he or she prepares to graduate from high school is a nice gesture. Your note may be welcomed in ways you never imagined.

Look around you now. Who is out there, beaming with good news?

★ ★ ★ ★ ★ ★ ★ ★

"Congratulations on a fine year scholastically. You can be proud of the effort you put forth, and I enjoyed watching you display the gifts God has given you. As you prepare for the rest of your life, may you choose wisely each direction placed before you."

"Tears came to my eyes when you were baptized. You have given your life to a worthy Savior. And aside from having a very special friendship with you, we are now sisters in Christ. I'm so happy for you."

"What wonderful news to hear of the birth of [baby's name]. I know your family is excited and thankful for the beautiful girl God gave you. May God's blessing give you joy in the years ahead."

"What great news! Ten years of service with [company]. This is a great accomplishment, and I am happy for you. As you continue working, may God give you many more years of productive service."

"We are happy to hear of your engagement to [name]. What wonderful news! Enjoy this time of planning and looking forward to the future that God has given you."

"I was glad to hear of your recent promotion to manager at the bank. I know you've worked hard to achieve this goal and you must be pleased with your accomplishment. Trust God to give you wisdom and direction as you learn your new assignment."

"God is not surprised by our circumstances, and I'm not surprised at your success! You have diligently applied yourself and are now reaping the joys of your hard work. It is something to be proud of."

"You've worked so hard on your new book, and now it's published. The time and effort you put into it was worth it! What a wonderful story. It's so good to read something that is uplifting. God has certainly gifted you in writing. I can hardly wait for your next book!"

"The dream has finally arrived! You're off to Spain to touch the hearts of those God has prepared for His special love. I am excited for you, and all the unexpected ways He will use you in the lives of others. Every morning know that "his compassions never fail" (Lamentations 3:21-26), and every evening as you lay your head down remember "your soul finds rest in God alone" (Psalm 62:1). He is faithful. May your heart know the fullest of His blessings as you serve Him in Spain."

"What lovely hats you knit for ladies going through chemo treatments! They are surely a treasure to each lady who receives one. Going through chemo is difficult enough, but losing your hair in the process doesn't help. Giving ladies these cute hats is a wonderful way of showing your concern for their well-being. I admire your sensitivity."

"Your graduation from high school is a great achievement, and soon you will leave for boot camp. What an adventure you are embarking on! I'm so proud you have chosen to serve our country. It takes a strong person to step up and strive for his or her best, as you are doing. I will be praying for you and trusting God will provide the courage and strength you will need to get you through training. Stand tall!"

"You finally made it! Retirement. I'm so happy for you! You have labored long in your chosen field and you can now reap the benefits of your hard work. What a great role model you've been to the children you've taught. Your lessons will linger long in their minds and help them to achieve success with their lives. Now it's time for you to relax and thank God for providing this special time."

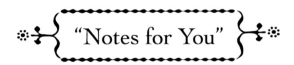

"Notes for You"

One morning last week I read a poem by Harriett Beecher Stowe. The first verse, especially the last line in that verse, touched my heart. "Still, still with thee, when purple morning breaketh, When the birds waketh, and the shadows flee; Fairer than morning, lovelier than daylight, Dawns the sweet consciousness, I am with thee." The first thoughts of Jesus, as we awake each day, are special. We are not alone … for God is with us. What a joyous way to begin a new day! Sweet mornings to you.

Have there been mornings when you awoke and the first thing you heard was the song of a bird? I silently smile as I lay in bed, enjoying the melody.

I want to have thoughts of Jesus first, but unfortunately, He's not always the first thing that comes to my mind. This is especially true on weekend mornings when my routine changes. Sometimes it's not until I start exercising that I remember to say: "Good morning, Father."

But some mornings I do remember God as my very first thought. I thank Him for my safety through the night, for good sleep, and that I don't have a headache! I acknowledge that He's in control of all things. I express joy regarding my salvation.

"Still, still with thee …" What a thought. God is never far away. He's always with me. Just a silent call is all it takes to be with Him. I depend on that. Always knowing that I'm not alone.

Yes, I strive to have Jesus be my first thought each morning and my last thought each night. But if it isn't, I know He is still with me.

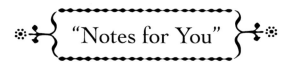
"Notes for You"

I have always been touched by Jesus' words in John 17, beginning at verse 20: "My prayer is not for them alone. I pray also for those who will believe in me through their message." Jesus prayed specifically for you and me. In verse 26 He continues: "That the love you have for me may be in them and that I myself may be in them." What joy to know Jesus prayed for us and loves us!

I just love it when someone tells me they prayed for me! And to know that Jesus prayed for me, too. Well that's encouraging!

Telling someone "I'll pray for you" is a very serious statement. I've found in writing encouraging notes that making that statement puts a "burden upon my heart." If I write it, I better do it.

I've always felt strongly about doing what I say I'll do. Whether it's "I'll call you," "I'll have you over," or "I'll send you" it weighs heavy on my heart until I have fulfilled my promise.

When I was a separated and then divorced mother, it hurt when someone said they would call and then didn't. Making idle commitments for conversation's sake has the potential to hurt someone who is already in need.

It's important to me that my word is true. Not only for the person to whom I give it, but it's important as a mature Christian. I'm reminded of Psalm 34, verses 12-13: "Whoever of you loves life and desires to see many good days, keep your tongue from evil and your lips from speaking lies."

Knowing Jesus prayed for me is awesome! I want to have that reputation.

Across the Miles

Missionaries are our brothers and sisters spreading the gospel of Christ at home and in foreign lands. Don't forget to make them a part of your note writing ministry as you reach out to encourage others.

A note to a missionary might include appreciation for their work, inspiration to trust Jesus for their needs, and timely news from the States. Mail call is a highlight in their lives.

Missionaries enjoy hearing about happenings at your home and news from your church. Many of our missionaries have only a handful of English-speaking associates to interact with. They will appreciate hearing about your life and family. This also gives them the opportunity to pray for you.

Missionaries face the same emotional and physical difficulties that we do, and many more! There are the usual illnesses, heartaches, and disappointments that all of us go through. But they also deal with difficulties common only to the land they are in, such as lack of medical care and unappetizing food.

Remembering birthdays and anniversaries is special. Holidays are important, too. Allow three or four weeks when mailing for a special occasion to ensure they receive it on time.

Consider writing or calling the parents of missionaries. The parents will be happy to hear that someone is praying for and writing to their children. Plus, they will probably have updated information to share with you.

Writing to a missionary is more than writing a note to encourage. When someone is away from home for three or four years at a time, a note from home is a joyful celebration.

★ ★ ★ ★ ★ ★ ★ ★ ★ ★ ★ ★ ★

"We hope you arrived safely in Bolivia, and you are beginning to settle in your new home. We know it will be awhile before your boxes are unpacked and a routine is established. As you adjust to your new home we will be praying for you and your family."

"We received your March letter and were happy to hear about the progress you're making in the work. Language study must be very difficult and we trust God is working in you to help you understand the language. We hope Alice recovered from her cold and that the family is well again."

"Our church family went on a retreat in the mountains over the Labor Day weekend. Our study was centered around prayer. Everyone enjoyed a beautiful weekend of fun and fellowship. We're thankful God allowed us the opportunity to hear His Word and enjoy a rest at the same time."

"The snow finally arrived here in Mt. Airy, Maryland! We knew you wouldn't believe the amount of snow we received, so the pictures we've enclosed tell the story. I lazed in front of the fireplace while Jerry had the chore of snow removal on the tractor. As you can see, it wasn't a chore to him—he loves 'riding the range' as he calls it."

"We trust all is well with you! Thank you for your recent prayer letter. The translation work seems to be going well. I'm sure it's a difficult job. We appreciate your obedience to God and thank you for serving Him."

"We prayed for you last night at our prayer meeting. We are proud to be partners with you in the work with the Ese Ejja people. You're not alone! God hears prayer and is watching over you."

"Thank you for your timely newsletters. It's a joy to hear about the work you're doing. We appreciate the time you put into writing the newsletters to keep us up-to-date. Thanks for considering us your partners in service. We keep you in our prayers."

"We're looking forward to seeing you soon. We trust your flight back to the States will go smoothly and your transition to the American way of life won't be a shock. Hopefully, your time stateside will be relaxing and encouraging. See you soon!"

"We continue to remember you in prayer as you study the tribal language. Don't be discouraged that it's taking a long time. You've chosen a special group of people to work with and they're just as eager as you are to be able to communicate. God is surely guiding your direction and His strength will help you get through this. Just think of how far you've come already! May your hearts be encouraged knowing we care."

"The skit you performed for our church was a real eye-opener to the life you live in Africa. It's hard to imagine the way people live in other countries. You opened our eyes and our hearts to the work you are doing. Please know that we will be praying for you and your family. You're in our hearts and we want to encourage you as you work to bring the gospel to others."

"We are thankful you were able to get to the city for the operation you needed. God's timing provided the doctor and nurses just when you needed them. He is always faithful! Let the brothers and sisters in China minister to your needs. Before you know it you'll be ready to return to the tribe and continue your work."

"We are so glad you will be joining our church family for the mission's conference in March. We are eager to hear about your first year overseas and all you've learned about your new country. The enthusiasm in your newsletters is contagious! We are so proud of the work you've chosen—to serve God overseas. Have a safe journey home and we will see you soon."

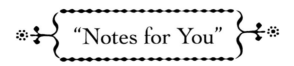

"Notes for You"

This week I watched two videos I haven't seen in a while. They tell of a tribe in South America that received Christ and has since taken the message of God to twelve other villages. My perspective of life here in the United States is kept in check as I consider the life of people around the world. We have been blessed with many riches. This is especially noticeable at Christmastime with all the gifts we purchase. I'm glad I could spend time watching God's work around the world. It keeps my mind focused on the only thing that counts—Jesus.

"Missions" is a very big part of my life. It wasn't until I married Jerry that I became interested in missions—carrying the gospel to the lost. He introduced me to a mission organization and the people he supports overseas.

Bringing the gospel to people in foreign lands is a long-term project. The native language must be learned; trust with the people must be built, and relationships must be made before one can begin to teach about God's love. Many years pass before their efforts return results.

I write the missionaries Jerry and I partner with at least four times a year, sending encouraging words to strengthen them and help them feel connected to their "former home in the States." I'm encouraged knowing that they pray for me and my family as I write them news about our life.

Just recently, Christy, who works with people in Mongolia with her husband, Dan, wrote and told me: "I think of you often as I have kept one of your note cards on my kitchen windowsill. I loved the one with the picture of the dairy cows and the barn, so I keep it there to look at and enjoy."

Something as simple as a note card with a scene from America is all it takes to touch someone overseas. What can you do?

We're all on mission for God.

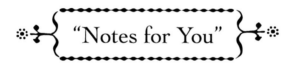

"Notes for You"

This morning, the title of my devotion message was, "A Heart That Won't Quit," and the scripture verse was Galatians 6:9: "Let us not become weary in doing good, for at the proper time we will reap a harvest if we do not give up." The message was just what I needed today. And God always plans it that way—to give us what we need to help us through each day. We must always keep our eyes on the goal, for that is what keeps us going through the good and bad. Our Lord refreshes us always!

My heart would quit often if I let it. I have a tendency towards depression and emotional upset, so life looks plenty glum to me.

During my season of hurricanes I often wanted to give up. Divorce and a prodigal child have been my ultimate traumas to live through so far. And many other small hurricanes that all of us go through in everyday life make it difficult for me to keep a smile on my face.

I'm thankful, though, that my faith is strong and my understanding of Scripture clear. Each morning I wake up to a new day of possibilities and an opportunity to show God's love through ways He's gifted me.

In Luke 18:5 we read of the woman who was persistent in her request for justice against her adversary: "Yet because this widow keeps bothering me, I will see that she gets justice." Because of her perseverance, the judge granted her request. I want to be like her—never giving up until the day Jesus calls me to His side.

"Keep your eye on the goal" is never far from my thoughts because hurricanes hit when I least expect them. By maintaining my routine and discipline each day of exercise and devotion time, my days don't just run smooth—they are smooth. I'm not running to God for help after a long absence. We're in touch during the good times and rough times.

The Adventure Begins

Is your heart stirred to write a note of encouragement? That's really the question. The insights I have provided won't be worth anything if you don't desire to encourage.

My heart is moved, and I hope yours is too. I like the proverb Solomon wrote that says, "He who refreshes others will himself be refreshed" (Proverbs 11:25). As Christians, God wants us to encourage one another. As we receive encouragement from His Word and promises, we pass it on.

I can't stop writing notes. When I stop to think about all the notes I've written, I wonder, "What if I never did? Would it have made a difference?" Nobody really knows but God.

I would be amiss if I did not mention the importance of prayer. Prayer always comes first. It is God's love we are reaching out with. We can be confident in writing the right words when we have His wisdom and guidance. Only through prayer can we hope to receive it.

Trust the words that come to you. My first impressions are usually the most suitable, and I accept that God has brought them for me to use. If you hit a snag and don't feel creative, as often happens to me, draw upon the examples mentioned in this book and find suitable sentences to put together. A proper note is soon on its way.

The year I wrote to the lady in my Sunday school class I made a copy of all the notes I'd written. Many times when I need something to say when writing to another person, I look at that collection of notes to help me choose the right words.

In "Billy Graham in Quotes," Mr. Graham said: "With an old head and a young heart, you can be a source of real strength [to others] who need your cheer and encouragement." I agree!

The opportunities are out there. They are waiting for you to find them. Are you going to begin?

Take the first step. God is ready to use you. He will stand by you in this new adventure for *it is an adventure*. God's ways are beyond our imagination. How wonderful to know He can use a note you've written to encourage and help someone else.

Remember, you must take the first step. Do it now. You **CAN** do it!

As Time Goes By

It's been many years since I wrote my first note. My pen hasn't stopped sending words of encouragement. From youth to adults to seniors, a note makes the same impression no matter the age.

I still sit down every Sunday afternoon to write notes. This is the time I've set aside to encourage the hearts of others. Sitting at my writing desk, I list those individuals who need a word of encouragement.

It takes discipline and time—as any other service does. But my heart never fails to come away refreshed.

Note writing *does* make a difference. People need encouragement, and people need to write it. This book can help you provide the encouragement others need.

I remember the words a woman sent me: "Don't ever stop using [your gift]. You don't know how much it meant to me." A victim of cancer, she was encouraged by my notes. What more meaningful service could I ever be doing for God?

It's time to sit down and write a note. As David Jeremiah said on his "WRITE Way to Encourage" CD, "Words are powerful." I hope you'll join me and be "NOTE" worthy for God!

Tips on Note Writing

A brief message from a loving heart can change a person's outlook.

Notes provide words of encouragement, not an opportunity to give advice or offer false hope.

Share from your heart ... you can be bold when you write.

If you write and say that you're praying for someone, do it!

The simplest words are the best.

Have good listening ears so that you are aware of a need.

Keep copies of the notes you write for a handy resource.

Writing notes is a heart issue, not a time issue—plan well.

Reserve a special time to devote to note writing.

Note writing will have a positive impact on your own life!

Keep note cards and paper in a place easily accessible to you.

When sending more than one note to a person, pull several different note cards from your collection so that each card will be different. This way your recipient will enjoy a different note card each time.

Resources

Books

Robyn Freedman Spizman. *When Words Matter Most: Thoughtful Words and Deeds to Express Just the Right Thing at Just the Right Time.* Crown publishers

Cheri Fuller. *The Fragrance of Kindness.* J. Countrymen, publisher

Florence Isaacs. *Just a Note to Say: The Perfect Words for Every Occasion.* Clarkson N. Potter, Inc., publisher

David Jeremiah. *The Joy of Encouragement.* Multnomah Books.Turning Point Ministries.

Henriette Anne Klauser. *Put Your Heart on Paper: Staying Connected in a Loose–Ends World.* Bantam Books, publisher

Joyce Landorf Heatherley. *Special Words: Notes for When You Don't Know What to Say.* Ballantine Books, publisher

Caroline Linse. *The Treasured Mailbox: How to Use Authentic Correspondence With Children, K–6.* Heinemann, publisher

Florence Littauer and Gay Talbott Boassy. *A Letter is a Gift Forever.* Harvest House, 2001.

Alexandra Stoddard. *Gift of a Letter.* Doubleday publishers

CDs

David Jeremiah. *WRITE Way to Encourage.* Turning Point Ministries.

David Jeremiah. *Onesiphorus–A Refreshing Friend.* Turning Point Ministries.

David Jeremiah. *How to be an Encourager,* Turning Point Ministries.

Florence Littauer. *Silver Boxes: The Gift of Encouragement.* CLASServices, Inc.

Charles R. Swindoll. *The Refreshment of Onesiphorus.* Insight for Living,

CPSIA information can be obtained at www.ICGtesting.com
Printed in the USA
BVOW071247120212

282728BV00001B/8/P

9 781462 400287